SPORTS SUPERSTARS

WHO IS PATRICK MAHOMES?

PERCY LEED

Lerner Publications ◆ Minneapolis

Stats in this book are accurate through the 2024 National Football League season.

Lerner Publications Company
An imprint of Lerner Publishing Group, Inc.
241 First Avenue North
Minneapolis, MN 55401 USA

For reading levels and more information, look up this title at www.lernerbooks.com.

Main body text set in Mikado.
Typeface provided by HvD Fonts.

Designer: Mary Ross **Photo Editor:** Evan Villas

Library of Congress Cataloging-in-Publication Data

Names: Leed, Percy, 1968- author
Title: Who is Patrick Mahomes? : Kansas City Chiefs superstar / Percy Leed.
Description: Minneapolis, MN : Lerner Publications, 2026. | Series: Lerner sports rookie. Sports superstars | Includes bibliographical references and index. | Audience: Ages 5–8 | Audience: Grades K–1 | Summary: "Three-time Super Bowl champion Patrick Mahomes is the face of the NFL. Learn about his life and find out how the Kansas City Chiefs quarterback became one of the most successful players in league history"— Provided by publisher.
Identifiers: LCCN 2025023077 (print) | LCCN 2025023078 (ebook) | ISBN 9798765689639 library binding | ISBN 9798348029135 paperback | ISBN 9798765697948 epub
Subjects: LCSH: Mahomes, Patrick, 1995- —Juvenile literature | Kansas City Chiefs (Football team)—Juvenile literature | Football players—United States—Biography—Juvenile literature | Quarterbacks (Football)—United States—Biography—Juvenile literature | LCGFT: Biographies
Classification: LCC GV939.M284 L44 2026 (print) | LCC GV939.M284 (ebook) | DDC 796.332092—dc23/eng/20250807

LC record available at https://lccn.loc.gov/2025023077
LC ebook record available at https://lccn.loc.gov/2025023078

Manufactured in the United States of America
1-1012764-54831-7/22/2025

TABLE OF CONTENTS

SUPER QUARTERBACK

The 2024 Super Bowl was in overtime. Quarterback Patrick Mahomes ran with the football.

He threw a pass. Touchdown! Patrick and the Kansas City Chiefs were Super Bowl champions.

Patrick was born in Tyler, Texas, in 1995.

His father was a baseball player.
Patrick loved baseball too.

Patrick played baseball, basketball, and football in high school.

After high school, Patrick went to college at Texas Tech. He played football and baseball there.

After two years at Texas Tech,
Patrick stopped playing baseball.
He focused on playing football.

In 2016, Patrick played his last game for Texas Tech. He joined the Chiefs in 2017.

In his first season, Patrick practiced and learned about the NFL. He played only one game.

In 2018, Patrick was his team's top quarterback. He helped the Chiefs win 12 games.

Patrick played in his first Super Bowl in 2020. The Chiefs faced the San Francisco 49ers.

The 49ers were ahead by 10 points. Then Patrick threw two touchdown passes. The Chiefs won the Super Bowl!

In 2021, the Chiefs reached the Super Bowl again. They lost to the Tampa Bay Buccaneers.

Patrick and the Chiefs beat the Philadelphia Eagles in the 2023 Super Bowl. They won again in 2024. They beat the 49ers by three points.

In 2025, the Chiefs reached the Super Bowl for the fifth time in six seasons. They lost to the Eagles.

Only three quarterbacks have won more Super Bowls than Patrick has.

Can Patrick and the Chiefs
win more Super Bowls?
Fans can't wait to see.

Patrick will keep working to be the best quarterback he can be.

PATRICK MAHOMES

CAREER STATS

GAMES PLAYED: 112

PASSING YARDS: 32,352

TOUCHDOWN PASSES: 245

RUSHING YARDS: 2,243

TOUCHDOWN RUNS: 14

PATRICK MAHOMES

GEAR

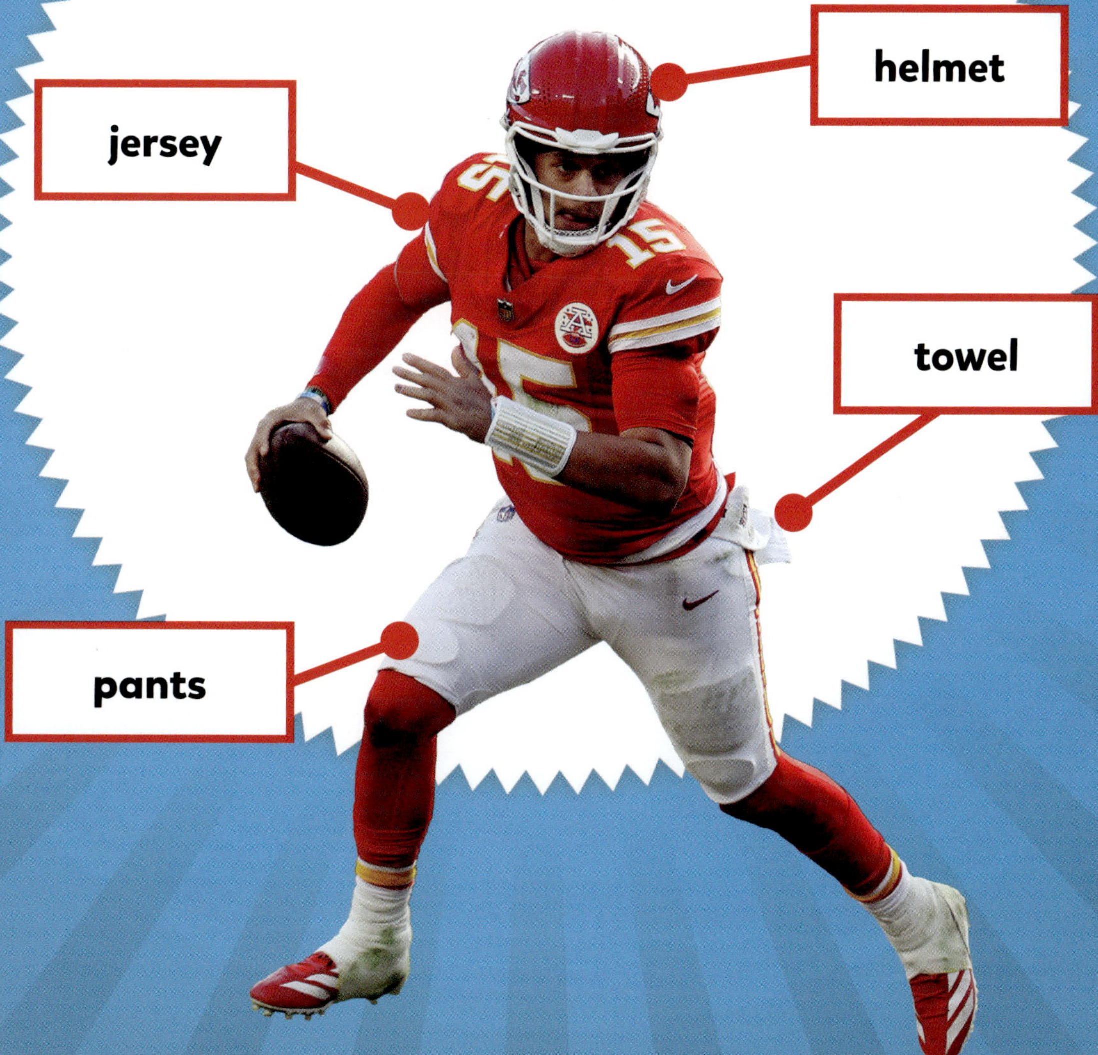

GLOSSARY

NFL: National Football League

overtime: time added to the end of a game when the score is tied

quarterback: a football player who calls the team's plays and throws passes

Super Bowl: the NFL's championship game

LEARN MORE

Leed, Percy. *Football's Super Bowl*. Lerner Publications, 2025.

Leed, Percy. *Football Superstars*. Lerner Publications, 2025.

Streeter, Anthony. *Super Bowl All-Time Greats*. Press Box Books, 2025.

INDEX

PHOTO ACKNOWLEDGMENTS

Image credits: Michael Zagaris/San Francisco 49ers/Getty Images, p. 5; Rich Pilling/MLB Photos via Getty Images, p. 7; John Weast/Getty Images, p. 9; Rich Graessle/Icon Sportswire via Getty Image, p. 11; AP Photo/Elaine Thompson, p. 12; ANGELA WEISS/AFP via Getty Images, p. 15; Ezra Shaw/Getty Images, p. 21; Jamie Squire/Getty Images, p. 19; Andy Lyons/Getty Images, p. 21; David Eulitt/Getty Images, p. 23. Design element: liangpv/Getty Images.
Cover: Cooper Neill via AP.